Dreamland, Somewhere Else

NEIL J. FOX

Independently published.

ISBN: 9781074977955

First Printing, 2019

To my parents – and the friends that stood the test of time, and those who didn't.

CONTENTS

'There is nothing noble in being superior to your fellow man; true nobility is being superior to your former self.'

— Ernest Hemingway

PART ONE
A HERO'S JOURNEY

CHAPTER ONE
ENTRANCE TO THE UNDERWORLD

Average Joe

There he goes, yes that's him
Alas, just another average Joe

A boy of simple recognition
No talent, acclaim or anything to show

Kudos aplenty, or a lack thereof
Just another guy lacking his godly glow

Easily forgotten as he fits to the mould
Level of talents recognised an all-time low

Content with life but only on the surface
The exterior facade his weakest of woe

Considered normal, whatever that is
A lack of substance from head to toe

Alone in the world or so he thinks
Longing daily for his very own beau

This specific individual you may not meet
But are more alike than you could possibly know

Loves Me, Loves Me Not

A flick of a petal, swallowing my pride
Deep in my soul the butterflies fly
Flustered, I take another breath

LOVES ME

A steady drive down the lane of despair
Crossing the hazy highway, I proceed with caution
Hairs on my neck stand stiff

LOVES ME NOT

I look to the sky in search of hope
Not a man of faith, but a believer in fate
Through the wild blue yonder, the cosmos are clear

LOVES ME

A realist approach to a surreal situation
Hope for the best, prepare for the worst
As a self-proclaimed realist, I admit my unreadiness

LOVES ME NOT

Crackhead

Higher than high
Craving your presence
Just a touch

No cause for concern
Looking for my next bump
Ready to make the jump

A non-negotiable deal
Light of my life
Colours other than blue

A natural state of euphoria
The source of my pain
Simultaneously my saviour

Adamantine addiction
A release of endorphins
Sick to my stomach

Authenticity

A dip of my toe into the known unknown
Creeping from the shadows, taking a mere peak

It comes to you over time, a cliché some might say
Sadly, as some never allow it to settle at all

Along the already rocky road you encounter disguised enemies
Attempting to drown you before you know how to swim

Burdened of your fabricated reputation
But instead allowing yourself to just be

Time and awareness become close companions
Enabling you to eventually swing the door open with force

If considered a witch, then burn me at the stake
As flames of my unapologetic authenticity will exhilarate

To both age and the senses, I hang up my coat
Swarmed in the midst of revelation

A Tale of Two Boys

Two hearts
One undeniable connection of chemistry
And an indestructible force that nothing can halt
This is the tale of two boys

A hate crime to the heteronormative
The sweet seduction of a second-class classification
Misunderstanding of a simple preference
As if a life-threatening condition

Hand holding in public
Indulging in the idea of a white picket fence
Simply existing in a world that we created
Happy together

A longing hope to be ignored
Wondering if heads will never not turn
A desire for a day that there will never need be
A tale of two boys

Man of Steel

A curse of kryptonite
What doesn't kill you makes you stronger
Still alive and growing powerless, on the contrary
A sucker punch to the soul, I'm losing strength

Merely mortal
A vessel of my being
Becoming deprived of my superpower to survive
Is anybody still inside?

Survival instinct
Through consistency of uncertainty
Considered a lover, with no alternative but to fight
Thickening of my skin as I turn to stone

As warmth leaves my body, I climatize
In my defence I have no control
I am not the chosen one as I needed saving
And sadly, I become a man of steel

The Universe

Riding the rings of Saturn
Existence through the Creation of Adam
Gravitational attraction binding the stars and dark matter
As time is the most powerful force of all

The most beautiful being we cannot touch
As our insignificance highlighted through our limitations
Deep seeded emotions and feelings are always valid
All in all, we still matter

We must learn to travel not only through time
Through space, humanity, mentality and understanding
For our existence is but a speck of dust
On the unopened wardrobe of opportunity

Enlightenment of a larger kind
Like the 10 billion light years lighting the abyss
We must all find our incredible and our beautiful
And let it shine through the darkest of times

Serendipity

Plunging through the depths of my deepest desires
Educating myself an earnest student

A cliché is a cliché for a reason
We need to learn to identify the source in stride

Familiar paths we can walk in the dark
And the shortcuts we create with the intent to survive

The only beliefs and opinions valued our own
In the knowing decisions made hell-bent for good

Surrounded by peers, acquaintances and strangers a plenty
And I'm going to enter talking

What was once my vice, is now my virtue
My superpowers the serendipity of my awakened soul

I take a seat in the winter of my coming of age
Going, going, gone -

CHAPTER TWO
FROM CALIFORNIA, WITH LOVE

Poolside

A bigger splash
Dive so deep I'm over my head
Kaleidoscope of blue
A fresh feeling of new beginning

The glistening chill of liberation
A fantasy
Some said would never come true
Part of the new classic

Flirting with success
Another concoction of juice
Feeling in the atmosphere
Anything is possible

A sense of sustainability
Reassurance to be rest assured
Floating above the surface
Holding my breath

Baby Pink Bonnet

Let's arise and go now
To where the sun shines bright in Nevada
90 miles per hour
The wind is strong
On the baby pink bonnet

Laughing hard and singing soft
My skin is hot
My feet not at all cool
The sun is soaring and watching
Over that baby pink bonnet

A look of reassurance
Glistening shades and a cracking smile
The indescribable feeling in my core
There's nowhere I would rather be
Behind this baby pink bonnet

The sun has set, or yet to rise
Glazing up at the night sky through double glazed glass
Dreaming, wishing and maybe hoping
For always night and day
Someday
Of that baby pink bonnet

City Star

Top of the world we're sipping red wine
A dream I never knew
Side by side we're together
Tomorrow I'm giving up, but not tonight

Glamorously gleaming and glistening
A dream come true
I understand, I'm not a fool
But I can feel the love tonight

A melting clock in Hollywood
Dali and Hockney combined
Window gazer, city escaper
Learning and dreaming at once
This whole new fantastic point of view
Is already coming to an end of its time

This city is crazy
And so am I, about you
Overlooking city stars in the city of stars
With you, a city star

Beverly Hills

Dreamy
Tall and beautiful
Shining bright
Beverly Hills

So pretty
Got it all
So they say
Beverly Hills

Enticing
Half full or empty
Anything at all
Beverly Hills

A good game spoken
Facade to be believed
Not anymore
Beverly Hills

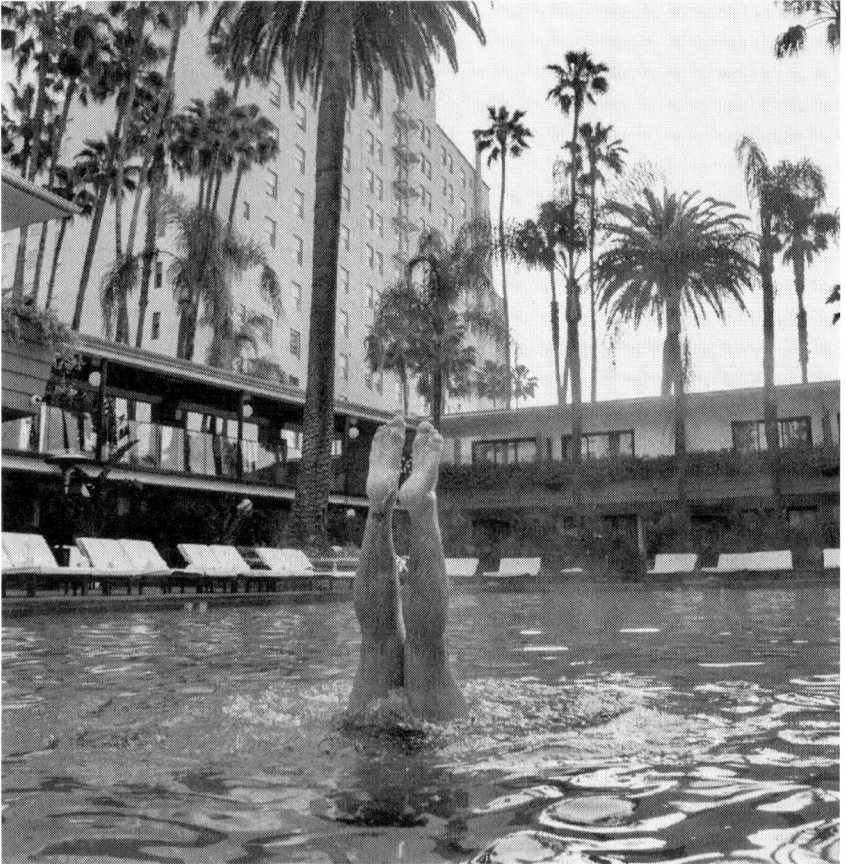

The Taste of Champagne

Moet Moet
Welcome to the Good Life
My inner desires electrified
Is this the taste of champagne?

We may never be royals
Golden elixir lines our throats
Not a celebration in sight
I love the taste of champagne

A victorious lap of luxury
We toast again, and again
Will it ever get tiresome?
The taste of champagne

Moet Moet
Crystal ball to the unforeseeable
Thirst quenched; taste buds teased
I've a thirst for more champagne

In Casablanca

Timeless classic retold
Emotion translates through era
Another time, place and soul
Something I've felt before

In Casablanca

Yet something significant is bubbling
A coincidence too coincidental
Nor do I believe in the Universe
I'm second guessing myself now

In Casablanca

Have a yen for Utopia
The crashing shores of Malibu
Or a stretch of streets through Dublin
Can reminisce time and time again
Of a crowded gin joint

In Casablanca

Just a Fan

Idolised lover
And a not so secret admirer
Artistic substance treasured
Collaborating feat on the horizon

A double-edged sword
Die-hard obsessed brainstorming for more
I suppress moments of anticipated bliss
Moves made calculated and adored

I never believed the city was haunted
Billboards modest, carpets faded
Hollywood Forever
A California summer never seemed so cold

An iron anchor for a heart
The coast clear, and dreary some
Memories inked like an autograph
As I'm reminded once more of my role

Dreamland, Somewhere Else

A window gaze embracing mindful desertion
Beige walls, a capsule filled with blue

Surrounded by belongings, lacking the sense
Not here but there, anywhere

The blanket of night darkens the street
Illuminates the manifestation of imagination

A yearning for escape, complete desperation
The pleading prisoner craving release

An unattainable dream now a regular reality
The clock spills wisdom, reflective of time

Desired destinations hold no coordinates
An inbound voyage greets a warm welcome

A dreamland, somewhere else

CHAPTER THREE
SPECULATION

Into My Own

A phoenix rising from the ashes,
Happened before and to come again,
Fall seven times, stand up eight

Memorable, but not so familiar
A place I've been before
Souvenirs and postcards not requested

The script word for word
I try to catch myself but I'm out of control
Speculation of a right move, I'll never know

Self-actualisation of an ever-changing man
Bullseye to a moving target
I aim, I aim again

The most qualified for the role
Needlessly reminded
This is what you came for

The curtains calling another time
This time I'm coming
Into my own

The Greater Gamble

All dressed up, ready to go
Yet things are moving slower than slow
A speedy start at a hesitating halt
Time and time, again
Push has come to shove
The dice rotates in a clenched hand
Sweating
The playing board and aspirations simultaneous
They are in clear sight
Pensive pondering of how simple it seems
How do so many others get by?
What seems like a headache puzzle
A walk in the park for others
Risking it all
The cards are dealt
I'm confident in my hand
I've got this one in the bag
Then as suspected
Gameplay alters the outcome
He couldn't read my poker face
Or so I thought
Suspecting more players entered the game
A full house
The game now playing in my mind
I fold again

Bite the Dust

10:41pm in London
Splash of emotion on a white linen canvas
Muffled TV sounds, echoes of cosmopolitan
Another one bites the dust

The protagonist has fallen
A round of applause for a great effort
An encore, a new cast will form
Another one bites the dust

Growing tiresome but I carry on
Previously ignored red flags wave strong
This time my prerogative
I'm going to bite the dust

Life imitates art
The Taking of Christ
Out of the doorway the bullets rip
Another one bites the dust

A cause for concern
A fixed target or running joke
And another one
You know how this ends

Safe Space

And I think of it
My little light up red runners
Making my mark on the planet
From the word go
Creating

Attempting to eliminate myself
Of subconscious conditioning from birth
Questioning everything
The bigger picture
The smaller print

Why two? Why three?
And even still, why me?
The thoughts that gather
In the magnificent wasteland
Of my safe space

Peace on earth
And I can't wait for heaven

Stranger Faces

I see your face
in strangers faces
Familiarity in unfamiliar forms
Adaption of the highest form

The darkest place
Is yet the most comforting
I live in my head
Wondering what's happening in yours

End of the world
Are you growing tired of my love?
By the way (I still love you)
Oh, lonesome me

Chiaroscuro
My riches are poorly
In strangers faces
I see your face

Diadem

Through animality and impurity
And confusion of thought, a man descends

A stroke of genius
A fitting ahead of my coronation of absolution

For our problems will be a freckle upon the foot of the Universe
A fraction to the ultimate ego

Achievement my crown of effort
The diadem of my thoughts

An outstanding revolution
A case of evolution for the mind of man

A coming of age we don't all come to see
In the end, our no longer phased beings will be set free

With self-control and resolution,
And considered thought, a man ascends

(For)ever Enough

Come see about me
Sitting here wondering what we were ever going to be
Lurking only leads to being let down
Speculation of your selfish actions
A simple act of self-sabotage

Ever enough, will I ever be?
Forever enough for a stranger to come

A longing for a solution
The equations and the sums all add up
Lying awake at night still trying to solve it all
Restarting over for a resolution
Right again, wrong answer

Ever enough, will I ever be?
Forever enough for a stranger to come

Playing a fool
Wondering my worth
You say one thing and mean another
Acting a messer and I'm the jester?
Here I stay riding the waves of wonder

Elixir

A recent discovery
Of true celestiality within a not so ordinary world
With sources few and far between

Reawakening more often required by the hero
Knowledge is power and insight is clear
Restarting of a story that never once stopped

Swimming in the sea highlights the vacancy of invincibility
Similarly sensed when speaking with you
Terrified to the core, yet giddy

Eager to explore endless possibilities
Petrified of the unknown and beyond controllable prospects
Emancipation from the status quo

Speculation will always exist
With repetitive experience we learn to leverage
To gain strength from a weakness

A being's origin is not a reflection of their outcome
Sincerity of a character's character, flaws and all
Revival of a better being

PART TWO
BOYS WILL BE BOYS

CHAPTER FOUR
DISTASTE FOR DESIRE

Hunger

The lonesome tiger preys across land
looking to pounce on the deer first-hand

Slithering through the grass the snake appears
a movement of their next meal causing sudden veers

Up above, the hawk stalks from the sky
the snake with no idea of its upcoming fate to die

Crocodiles emerging from the lake for their next feast
already targeting an unsuspecting wildebeest

And the spider designs the most beautiful art
a stunning trap to tangle the fly and outsmart

The wolf lurks through the darkness of night
ending the life of the hare remaining out of sight

A cheetah bolts as quick as the flick of the wrist
the starving cat becoming the king of the forest

The chameleon changes the colour of his skin
a survival instinct, now the nearby rock his twin

We do what we have to do to get by
living in this world, eye for an eye

We are led by hunger to succeed and strive
the ultimate life goal is simply to survive

I Bought You A Mirror

Something selfless for the selfish
Pondering what it may take
Infatuated with an image over reality
Convincing me worthy of your presence

A gift for the self-proclaimed gifted
Spending a surplus of my time
Wealth depleted of an irreplaceable currency
In exchange for simple mutual connection

A blindingly shining awakening
Awareness in the reflection of your actions
The perfect attempt for my final plea
I bought you a mirror

Perceptive Dissonance

Perception is reality
Reality is what we know to be true
If knowing to be true is what is defined
Then my interpretation of love in life exists in you

To be considered normal
Conforming to a standard, usual, typical or expected
Is conditioned from our culture
A redefining of our definition can be resurrected

What do I know to be true?
Everything I see, all that I do
As we break down the character traits of our being
Our position shifts in lieu

A table is tangible
Emotions running through my system are not
The senses of human nature
Considered to be an afterthought

My understanding is that our understandings differ
What's normal is normal, to someone who deems it normal
We celebrate individuality as individuals
Yet agree over the idea of becoming conformal

We are but a manifestation of our environment
To describe oneself is to describe what one has been exposed to
We are but fabricated and manipulated beings
With no other choice but to live as we do

Culture is man-made
If holding similar beliefs in unison from inception
Through decades and centuries combined
Then I would never hold dear my perception

Godspeed

We crossed paths
Intersected each other's stories
On our own individual journeys

We played our roles well
A side character to the main tale
A minor blimp in the major scale

We learnt from each other
Taught lessons to help us on our way
Adding some colour to shades of grey

Filling in the blank
A useful resource for each other
Our wings eventually spread and flutter

And no longer we're in touch
Similar in styles we were sure enough
Two diamonds in the rough

Grateful for the time we had
I hope I planted a memorable seed
And with that, I wish you well

- Godspeed

Gargoyle Gates

At the foot of the steep winding hill
The gargoyle gates stand powerful and strong
Warily watching over the remote grounds
Seeking prey in that that doesn't belong
Playing warden like a loyal watchdog
The guardians from darkness don't rest
Patrolling the realm for potential destruction
Of stone and marble they stay perpetually abreast
Their great grey wings expand far and wide
Aged horns atop their head made of sharpened rock
Terrifyingly unnerving to even the most evil
Ready to savage intruders and unwanted flock
Many fear the gargoyles are too intense
The walls too high and cinder block thick
But when the walls were down last
Trust was compromised
Leaving no choice but to triple the brick
It's important to realise they'll never attack
Their purpose to protect from all that is tense
The gargoyles sit at the foot of the steep winding hill
Safeguarding for me
In my defence

Planet Earth

The grass beneath my feet
Our precious and remarkable land
Looking for the respect it deserves
At mercy to the litter-filled hand

The elixir of the earth
Coming from the wide and wondrous sea
Its lifespan becoming an egg-timer
Filling with plastic and even more harmful debris

Home of all beautiful living creatures
Their existence seen in the mass like a novelty
Co-existing on this planet together
A world free from animal cruelty

A look back at the man in the mirror
Ideas of social justice our implanted botany
A desire for living together harmoniously
The utopia of human equality

Pegasus

Personality brimming
Of confidence and kindness
Living like it's your full final day
Of your extraordinary life
An immortal winged horse

Never allowing yourself
To lead a little life
When inside you there is so much more
That won't never go unused
And never will be

Sometimes I think you see yourself
As a dark horse
Unaware of the light you bring
Inspiring me and others to shine
Bright like never seen before

Why do we get all this life
If we don't ever use it?
Why do we get all these feelings
And dreams and hopes
If we don't ever use them?

This transcendent place
Where angels, gods & saints reside
Be enthroned, or live
Is evident in your presence
Doing our best
To enjoy this remarkable ride

In a world of stallions and unicorns
Like lightning to a dark and dreary day
One thing is for sure
You are Pegasus

Regret or Relief

Be careful what you wish for
The need to have something special
The want for memorable events
Become an unhealthy obsession to the core

And when it's all over
We wonder was it really worth the hype
To be truly good as what it seemed
Achievement of our aspirations redeemed

An underwhelming sense of relief
Questioning of our actions and own intent
A build-up of our expectations
Of which would never have been a belief

Gaining a grasp on the foundation of our motives
Likelihoods of quixotic assumptions
An unconscious cause for upset
The overwhelming feeling of regret

Notions of wanting what we can't or just had
Our desires leading to self-destruction
Disregarding the outcome or aftermath of our actions
Leaving us sombre, and remorsefully sad

CHAPTER FIVE
HOLOFERNES

Thin Ice

The blistering cold ground
Meets the warmth of my sole
Trembling, steady and slow
Cracks in my assurance become certain

A ticking time bomb
Echoes of pandemonium nearing
Yellow, red, blue or green
Too late to trigger

I drew the short straw
Settled my fate and it's short-lived
Life support to the already lifeless
The camel lays still on the arctic terrain

Eggshells built from the beginning
The indisputable crunching of promises breaking
I continued to walk out to the middle of the lake
Always somehow knowing it was going to fall

Slits to the skin sink deeper
Deafening of the drums
The scars of the landscape disseminate
Shattering from beneath me

Down the Line

The deceleration of a truth-less oath
A gleam of faith for the futile

Catch you on the flip side
Down the line

Led towards the trail less travelled
Unanimity of an ill-will consensus

We'll meet beyond the bounds and borders
Down the line

I'll sit and wait by the wishing tree
The newest resident of a fool's paradise

On the dark side of the moon
Wishing and waiting for one more time

Down the line

A Regretful Regurgitation

I grab my throat, in horror and shock

A spewing of honesty onto your uninvited lap

Immediate penitence spills into the atmosphere

A look on my face of disappointment and upset

I wish, I could and I would take it back

The regretful regurgitation I couldn't control

Changing everything, begging to retract

Speaking on how I feel, an immediate qualm

I convince myself, that things will get better past night

A beautiful misconception of hindsight

Holofernes

We cross paths in all walks of life
The man, the myth, the legend
The abuser of power, in desperate seek
A cunning breed of sorts

Sitting at the head of the table
Unaware of justice, waiting to be served
A chalice filled with your own
Just desserts

A strong source of self-destruction
The unbeknownst suicide mission
A blissful beheading of ignorance
And the suited execution of selfishness

And again you will lose one's head
Whether it be from me or you
Hunger for retaliation engorged as
What goes around will come swinging with force

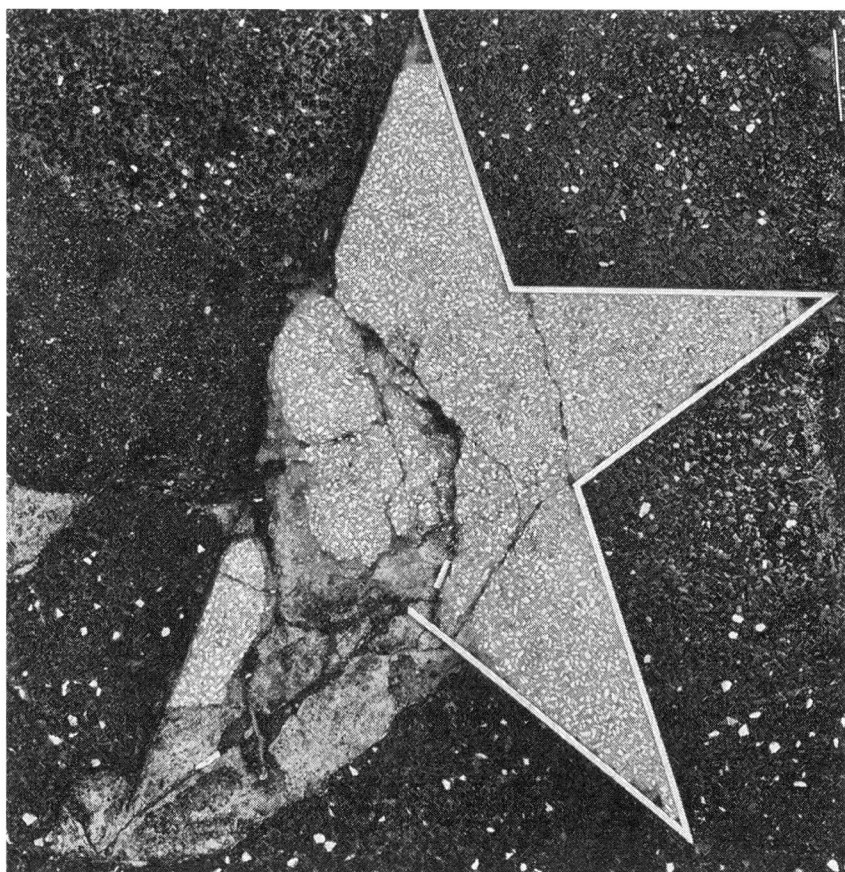

Sore Loser

It's sweet to taste, your bitter failure
Not by some misfortune or even bad luck

Complaining and blaming others for your loss
A fair and square trial, no forfeit in sight

And the days to come filled with morbid regret
Angered easily by a difficult defeat

A sore winner has fallen, what were we to expect?
An attitude less graceful was imminent no less

Deepest sincerity offered towards your defeat
You won't get your way for once, a tough bite to eat

Remembering to not celebrate those you hate
It's easy to become those we don't anticipate

Taken into consideration, I offer my condolences
And better look next time, my sweet sweet inferior

3 Wishes

III

I plea for your respect of one's community alike
Giving consideration to the culture
To those who will and won't cross your path

II

I ask that kindness is given to oneself
That you will tend to and care for the lone flower
And blossom into the greatest burst of bloom

I

I wish for your satisfaction with decisions made
When you close on the final chapter
You will be fulfilled with the choices paged

The Beautiful Misconception of Hindsight

We look back on the past
Living in a dreamland
Seeing things as better than they were
Life as we once thought we knew

Reminiscing in retrospect
Embarrassed of ourselves, what a shame
Holding us accountable for our actions
Admired apparitions running in parallel

Hindsight, the beautiful misconception
Planting flowers to the badlands
We add colour to the outlines of history
A rainbow dazzling through what was
Once a storm ridden sky

The Blank Stained Canvas

I pull out my blank stained canvas
And try to wipe away the marks
Diluting the damage of previous remarks

The stains stand stubborn
Hidden some and evidently present at times
Regardless, I carry on

A flicker of my brush
Starting to lay new foundations
My longing vision still strongly in mind

Layers thicken as time stretches
I hang my painting pride of place
Knowing what's hidden still behind the walls

CHAPTER SIX
HERE'S TO YOU, KIDDO

Chasing Dragons

I want to have the shiniest car
red, silver, green or gold
as long as it's fast and loud and low down
to the ground so when people see it
and hear the sound
they will know it's me coming

The house I will have is going to be huge
with a big massive roof that towers over the brick completely
and to get to my house will be this long winding road that's so long
it would nearly give you a headache
with lamp posts the whole way to the door that are beaming
up from the stone floor
people are going to wonder who lives there

My wife will be beautiful beyond belief
and my kids are going to think I'm the greatest dad ever
because I'm going to play with them all the time even when I'm tired
on their games or whatever they have then in the future
like robots or things that fly in the sky
I just want to be that guy that everybody will see
and turn to each other in jealousy to say
he must got it so good

Nostalgia

A moment of unanticipated transit
Sparking our memory of a place we have already been

Detecting images of visible light, of likeness
With electrical nerve-impulses striking us as once again seen

The assertion of odour molecules clouding the air
An accumulative haze of a previously-accustomed scene

Being able to identify a taste all that familiar
Playing reminder to a time few and far between

A perceived sound through detected vibrations
Forcefully guiding us towards a remembrance held keen

Activating pressure receptors held in the skin
A conscious contemplation of a fondling convene

The unwilling traveller transported through space and time
Guilty of a retrospective crime of what has or could have been

Hollyweird

The glorious sun
Lining the streets like glitter
Beaming through windows as fiery torches
Heating up the paths and plants

The trees extended 100 feet high
Fronds growing from the crown wide
Crashing against each other in the wind
Swaying back and forth in a dreamy-like fashion

The pools are as deep as the trees are tall
An underwater dream world I've dreamt in sleep
Swimming in slow motion, strokes and all
Under the water nobody can hear you singing your songs

The streets and the sky are at war
Together they're counting who holds the most stars
Surrounded by inspiration and beauty
Remembering to count your own ones too

And everyone there has their own unique style
Pink mow-hawks spiked to the sky
Skating down the polished pavement
Kickflips and coffee all day long

Every corner I'll pass it's clear
Seventh heaven will be a place smack bang right here
Overlooking the sign that this will be normal
Fitting in nicely will be even more weird

Doll Boy

People laugh when they see
He, who is playing with the 'girls' toys
Making up imaginative stories and playing free

Quietly brushing their hair
And putting on the latest fashion
The boy and these dolls a godforsaken pair

Chronicling lives with complex tales
Throwing them from the shelf to the blazing fire
A streak of masculinity veils

Interested in castles and lands of magic
Keeping himself enchanted
Elders look on feeling less than tragic

Dolls won't make him any less of a gent
Looking past the standard stereotypes and you'd see
A boy who simply could not be more content

The Darkness

A sweet embrace
Ignites the darkness
Freeing me from my fears
Flashes of complete starkness

The monster under my bed
Is trying to outdo and fool me
Transforming into a great big anaconda
Catching my jolting leg as I attempt to flee

The only light source that of the bathroom bulb
As it's past midnight and my bladder full
The demon at the bottom of the stairs waiting
For me to open the door for him to grab and pull

A hooded fellow hiding around the corner
Ready to pounce making his identity known
To use and do with me as he pleases
Of my bones he'll make his throne

Faces in the frames follow me with their eyes
Their features melting the longer they stare
Sprinting and panting, I bolt on by
Through the crack of the door I feel their glare

A martyr to my own imagination
Worry and voodoo considered sisters not twins
Of my own mind I easily fall victim
Befriending the unknown for all my sins

Another Slice of Toast

Jolting closed the door
Keeping out the rain
The wet seeped through to my socks
My feet cold again
Treading through the river-like town
A journey that felt like it would never end
Through the blistering cold we fought the wind
Puddles aplenty with my pockets zipped

Fresh cotton and linen line my skin
Warming up now and feeling myself again
I hear the kettle let out it's roar
Bundled onto the couch tired and sore
Asking when's dinner my stomach is empty
A clutter of cups I hear something coming
Hot chocolate and toast
My tiny belly lets out its last rumble

The television volume spikes for the ads
Causing ructions to my unintended slumber
I toss and turn on the comfortable couch
Bundled into what feels like a kangaroos pouch
Warm and snug I switch sides
In the process making some exaggerated noise
In a hope it'll be clear that I'm awake
Another slice of toast she'll know to make

Gladiator in Training

Skidding across the great hall
Trying to anticipate the next move
Like a ninja stuck to the wall
A gladiator in training

Climbing the mountainous chair
Sweat dripping from my temple
The red gladiator in complete despair
On my tail the entire course

Tip-toeing across the tight rope
The lava bubbling beneath
My opponent beginning to interlope
Losing my balance out of sheer panic

And then my final match
The coach who taught me everything
This chick is training to hatch
Making my best attempt to triumph

Now the graduated contender
In search of his own in Shangri-La
With goals made up of absolute splendour
The student has become the master

Learning

A promise to making smarter decisions
Removing emotions from the situation
Waiting until tomorrow
And knowing my own worth

The extra effort to be honest, but kind
Understanding that perception is reality
Awareness of the long-term effect of my actions
While minding my own business

That I have a choice to be miserable or be motivated
Identifying my vices, and limiting them
Utilising available resources to the best of my ability
And to leverage my responses effectively

I'm going to listen and ask more
Talk less about myself
To prioritise my privacy as modesty is sexy
I will appreciate and create more art

Needing to understand the difference
between want and need
Are you on the right path for where you want to be?
Practising to the best of my ability self-control
Asking questions like 'how is this really effecting me?'

Happiness is not a final destination
If it takes less than a minute, do it now

To live life a little less hectic
Plans should only be seen as a suggestion

To be more proactive and less reactive
Nobody else really cares about your goals
Turning your thoughts into ideas and actions
I need to step up for the starring role

Every day I am learning
Picking off apples from the knowledge tree
And if I continue to nurture my appetite
Then I am simply the best that I will ever be

PART THREE
WAR OF THE WORLDS

CHAPTER SEVEN
THROUGH THE CRACK OF THE EMERALD STONE

Boomerang

Do what you love and love what you do
And the world will come boomeranging back

The laws of cause and affect
If initiated correctly, full circles to you

An equivalent and opposite reaction for every action
Benefiting from the garden of which you sowed

Living by the principle of an unfulfilled prophecy
The deeds and words will soon recur

To celebrate the coming of the Prodigal Son
Because once lost, he is now found

And just like a boomerang If to leave once more
Without a shadow of a doubt, I'll return once again

Summer Solstice

A celebration of the sun
Utter joy spread and exposed to everyone
True representation of ascension

New seasons showcasing immense beauty
Ushering in the new light of nature's bounty
Awareness to all the good around me

Stopping to the smells of roses, and I will
Speculation of a right move
I suddenly know to be true

Longing for you in the dark nights
Knowing you would come, impatient still
We had the stars, you and I

A time of new beginnings with more to unfold
Illumination triumphs over darkness
Light of my life

The Last-Born Tod

What does it mean to be the last born Tod?
Holder of the pen to the future kin
The creator of life to continue a legacy on
Or the God of death to dwindle it all

Difficult it is, to imagine an unwinding road
To imagine just how far back the history goes
To see each face of ancestry gone
Watching over as I carry the crest strong

Walking through the forest filled with fear
Swinging the axe to the tree so greatly grown
Year to year, the branches and roots stemmed long
A fall from grace, pinned as all my fault

Then again, the halter of heritage may not sound so bad
To bequest the power to put it all to an end
Knighted for eternity as the final bearing progeny
O, what a wondrous victory that would be

Big 'Ol Private Joke

To be born and bred in deep green roots
Is to be in on one big 'ol private joke
A kinsmanship and community of a different kind
Pointing in hysterics as the world goes by
A deeper understanding into the depths of the world
With an acuteness and wit unmatched by neighbouring foes
A tiny land with a magnificent footprint among our toes
Duplicated but never replicated, never a truer word
Cause everyone wants to be in on the antic
Every year without fail, they pledge their allegiance
To us, the most wanted and claimed group there was
Coming from a place where "No Irish allowed!"
To turning rivers and buildings green in a plea for consent
Cheering among us not knowing what's really happening
And the world can continue to try to take part
At the end of the day, we know what we know
We will continue to go about our small island days
Making waves in the world and laughing along the way

Emerald

Rich and distinct
High of value
And soothing some

The embodiment of patience
A compassionate carer
Mental clarity and focus

Freshness and vitality
Unconditional love, unity full
The bringer of luck

Good fortune a plenty
Reasoning and spirituality
And wisdom galore

Rarer than rare
The deepest of hue
My pact to you

Homegrown Love

The curtain dances in the draft as the wind creeps in
What feels like a beam of fire freeing the world from sin
To the left, the tiny red light on standby shines
In my sanctuary of warmth stacking the pillows high
The comforting heat a spell, making me drift on by

And the ticking clock in competition for distraction
The duck feather duvet sound proofing from impaction
The wood is creaky and conducts its recital
Funny from such a sound, the composer so blatantly obvious
For the unwilling audience remaining oblivious

The window gazing out into the world going by
And the stars and street lights stare right back and spy
I switch over, flipping the pillow to its colder side
The familiarity of belongings, surrounded in the well-known
With a grown appreciation for home

Mother

Something to be said about a mother's touch
The most beautiful of spirit on this godly earth
A powerful creature, the creator of life
Supreme being, of divinity high

A nurturing care, comparable to none
The almighty minder, our mothering mum
Loving and kindness to all coming her way
The presence of sense to all madness led stray

But mother can be a sensitive soul
And is ageing as days go by and getting old
We must do what we can to keep her fresh
And as our duty, out of clear respect

The deed of life is unrepayable for us
Doing our best, being conscious of our tread
To be sensitive, kind and giving back
Look after and keep safe the cradle of life

Tír na nÓg

Legend says there is a place, beyond the western sea
Appropriately crowned, the land of the young
A place where age was never a fear
With skies bluer than blue and trees even more green

Where on land and sea, white horses run free
Across the golden shores of Tír na nÓg
A magical place of fawns and fairies
Residing among the few living harmoniously

Through the morning mist, the sunshine rose
Every day, what felt like summer solstice
The hills grew high and the grass long
A place some couldn't even think to dream at all

Not always I make it to Tír na nÓg in a day
As often creatures come trying to pull me away
Tripping and stumbling to make it across the hill
Every morning, my aim is even just to try and see it still

CHAPTER EIGHT
THE BULL AND THE ROOSTER

XXVI

Another the wiser
Wondering if I've grown stronger
On to the next one
No rest for the wicked

Clasping my boots
Preparing for the next battle
Releasing a sigh of relief
We made it this far

Knowledge is power
Ignorance is naivety
Calmness held to a higher regard
And silence golden

Respect and gratitude shall flourish
Self-control is arduous
Growth is imminent
I will be stronger

Tough Love

I hand you the pill
You find tough to swallow
I tried my best to spoon feed you
Spitting it out every time still

Tough love

I offer it honest and upfront
You reject, again
Leaving a bad taste in your mouth
I willingly force it upon you blunt

Tough love

I hope my vision will be clear someday
The struggles I've tried to make you see
My efforts in leading you down the right path
By walking away

Tough love

What It Means to Be a Champion

What does it mean to be a champion?

The superior, undefeated and truly out of this world

To be a champion of myself

Supporting and rooting for my own success

Allowing yourself to be confident but not cocky

Graciously outdoing my own efforts and abilities

Being an example of humbleness and modesty in victory

Level-headed and down to earth

If I am to wear the crown with honour

It will be because I have outdone and become my own successor

So, what does it really mean to be a champion?

To be supporting, challenging and becoming victorious

Both for and against one's self

I Will

I will nourish my mind
Be empathetic to my thoughts
And a therapist to my own feelings

I will build my body strong
Assemble a shrine of health
Something of which to be worshipped

I will fuel my spirit
And promise to pray for my soul
Being true to my inner being always

I will cater to my whole self
Creating circumstances which to burgeon
To the moon and back

MY MOTHER SAID TO ME,
"IF YOU ARE A SOLDIER,
YOU WILL BECOME A GENERAL.
IF YOU ARE A MONK, YOU
WILL BECOME THE POPE."
INSTEAD, I WAS A PAINTER,
AND BECAME PICASSO.
PABLO PICASSO

The Stubborn Sea Captain

There once was a stubborn sea captain
Sailing through the storm wearing proudly his gold clothes-pin

He liked to do things his own way
No member of crew on board could be of any help or have a say

Opinionated a plenty, on how the seas should be tackled
The talents of the crew on the operation of the ship left shackled

The stubborn sea captain passed judgement on his pirates
Definitive statements in passing on their character often lead to riots

Cause it was clear to him that no one could be as good as he
Yet none would get the chance to even see if they could be

A perfectionist with an ego as tall as the mast
No room for rigging as self-considered the best in all deck's past

The stubborn sea captain couldn't see that they were only trying to help
Getting involved and playing their part with the deadly storms dwelt

When one day he finally discovered the woes of his ways
The maps towards his treasures became much less of a maze

Goodwill Cunning

People look to the fox and call him cunning
Shrewd and slick in their ways
The dog skilled in achieving one's ends by deceit
Preying and planning and left lurking in the street

To be considered cunning is less than favourable
Devious some, in seek of defeat
Crafty and cute, and not in the good way
The artful pup often led astray

A credible misunderstanding of determination
Or a strong-willed animal approach to success
With purposeful intent
Useful traits to progress could remain unspent

But if the end justifies the means
Good outcome excusing the wrongs to initiate it
Fancy footwork used to entertain rather than bluffing
That to me, is goodwill cunning

War of the Worlds

In the midst of smoke and debris
I rise up from my knee
Getting my balance and wits about me
Slowly taking in my surroundings

The landscape swamped with grey
A bleak dark red sky conceals the fray
Blood shed is imminent
Playing witness to the battle at play

Clashing, of what seems like a thousand swords
A battle so otherworldly
Even the planets are colliding
I fall to avoid the arrows shot forward

In the mix up and scuffle of bodies aplenty
Bullets swerve past in this great manic frenzy
Utter destruction to the universe known
The rival cavalries disputing with blows

In the darkened day, it's clear in sight
A bull and a rooster
Scrapping through the night
Wounding each other 'til death is ripe

To my left, a pack and a troop
Tearing one another arm and limb
What looks to be a fight for the right
To lead, to seek, to take centre flight

The participants grow wounded
Carnage inevitably escalating
To an almighty melodramatic climax
An inauguration of the winner leads on

When the smoke has cleared
I am the last standing
Hostility has entered it's hibernation
I take a deep breath and sit in reflection

And just as I begin to enjoy the calm
The serenity of the land at last
Grateful, for my now clear head
I see the battalion rise again from the dead

Sunflower Fields

Garden of Eden
With a population of one
And the thousands of seeds I've sowed
Sprouting into flowers imitating the sun

An aim for adoration
Across acres of grass my allegiance loyal
I walk the lengths of the land watering daily
Building a heavens made for longevity

My planting regime to be admired
A substantial dedication for the roots of my soil
The fountain of youth, I hope to build
This life worth living won't go unfulfilled

Laying in the fields of my legacy
Protective of my offspring, quite literally
I have and will reach the rill of Nirvana
My promised land

CHAPTER NINE
WASTELAND

Back to California

When the sun sets in the west
I'll go back to California
Laying leisurely and still on the sandy beach
Silently admiring the diamonds of the sparkling sea

Blinded by the light of tranquillity and peace
I can see the world from here
A viewpoint I will everlastingly take advantage of
This, my happy hunting ground

In the history books of my family name
I'll be christened Icarus
Forever flying too close to the sun
Always your Angeleno

And when the sun rises in the east
Like clockwork
Drenching the days ablaze with orange
You'll know where to find me

David

Here before
And here more will come
The past is my present
A situation of inseparability
Experiencing this moment in time
An intimacy of crossed paths
Destiny unfolding through paper pools

They say life imitates art
Here, I will attest
My own animate existence knowing the score
Material works are more than an influence
In the beginning, there was only art
And nature it's guided disciple

Reincarnation of a unique kind
The living unified through resurrection
Through the rebirth of story, not soul
Consider this my coronation as the second king
The hierarchal samsara
And to those who will come after me
Well, here's looking at you

When the Sun Sets on Sunset

When the sun sets on Sunset
We watch the fall of fragile man as the seven crawl

From seeking beyond one's need
Believing that of which a requirement to succeed

To those who conduct a comparison of sorts
Sinking slowly into the sea of green

Acting intensely in their most convincing role yet
The scale grounded on validation, burying them underneath

And no concern held for the apathetic
As the weeds will succumb the disengaged buds

And we can't not hear the loud roar of the lion
Echoing a spurn-filled sorrowful plea, if you listen closely

Retaliation is a matter of time to the vengeful
In a vicious cycle of violent poetic justice

As for the self-diagnosed deficient
Alas, the insatiable look after themselves

And then there are those who have learned to conquer control
Frivolously dancing on the moon not afraid to fall

Picture Perfect

Living a fantasy
The immaculate impression
Life as we know it
A flight of fancy

Pressure makes diamonds
A confinement of the mind
What is supposed to be
Crumbling through vain expectation

Reaching for the moon
Storming the ladder
Desperate to simply be
Building castles in the air

Rewarding of the highest efforts
If indefatigably chasing
A life made that others will see
Picture perfect

Poolside Pt. II

Submerging from the dreamy depths
Panting, heaving, gasping
Satiety, starving for more
Plummets delving through the portrayal

Far beyond wild
Levelled up ten-fold
If happiness is power, then me
The most powerful man in the world

Mesmerising sisters work hand and foot
White frocks frolic with the wind
Rosé diluting rapidly
O, what a fortunate misfortune

A knowing touch
Grounds haunted with history
Wise winks met with a simultaneous smile
Alive again

Ferris Wheel

In the pit of my stomach

I foresee my prophecy steering south

When an eery silence swamps the surroundings

A breathy snigger pierces the atmosphere

A longing look overflowing in let-down

Is followed up with a slow modest smirk

The built walls of frustration

Annihilated through the winds of affirmation

When the storm of insecurity finally strikes the village

The conjuration of assurance casts over the sky

And when I start to look back up

The kaleidoscope of butterflies fly free

The Ballad of Peg Entwistle

Dear darling Peg
And now the Lord with thee
Blessed is the passion to which you lived
And sacrificed in the name of your art

To be remembered in perpetuity
A desire to succeed held to the highest
Alive through a Great Depression
The irony of which a humorous affair

We are all afraid, and often cowardly
A slave to our own expectations
Conscious of every one of our actions
And the effects they have on those around us

Now, since that historic day in Fall
A determined stride through Beachwood Drive
Thy Kingdom has come
And you will live on forever

Wasteland

Another sole's treasure
Cheating death, the life raft
Sailing and shoring

Bumps and bruises aplenty
Thrown to the wolves
There are two sides to every sword

Experience to be admired
The card-less sleeve
Image of the invisible

Beauty to the imperfections
Surface level scenarios
Looking beyond the landscape

You may say I'm pushing up daisies
I see lilacs out of the dead land

Thank you for making it to
the end of Dreamland.
I wrote this book as a means
to understand myself and learn
to be better.
At most, I hope that this
book made you think about
life and your own perspective.
　　　All my love,
　　　　Neil X

THE
Hollywood
Roosevelt

DREAMLAND, SOMEWHERE ELSE

Dreamland, Somewhere Else is a collection of poetry telling a story of self-discovery and betterment. The poems within this book share a common theme of self-realization and the idea of becoming the hero of your own story. The book details the trials and tribulations both internally and externally that we face taking on this role as the hero of our own stories, whether it be other people, worldly temptations, or simply down to our own character vices and virtues. It's the story of the evolution of a modern man and the internal struggles we can face as we take on this change.

The idea behind Dreamland, Somewhere Else is about how we, as humans, tend to fall victim to the term 'The grass is always greener on the other side'. When it's summer, we wish it was winter. When it's winter, summer and so on. 'If I had this, I would really succeed. If this, was this way...' etc. This is about self-discovery and realizing that the hand we were dealt is everything that we need in order to succeed. That we are the protagonist of our own journey and story, and that we need to believe in ourselves in order to progress and evolve and become the person that we were destined to be, while also accepting ourselves wholeheartedly.

ABOUT THE AUTHOR

Born and raised in Galway, Ireland, Neil J. Fox is a native of the West of Ireland and has always been involved and interested in art and its many forms, coming from a creative family. Having emigrated to the United States twice, Neil has experienced what is widely considered 'The American Dream', having lived in the picturesque Hollywood Hills.

Currently residing in Dublin, Neil is an experienced Marketing Manager with multiple years' experience within the tech industry, promoting high-end products and managing targeted campaigns for a growing client-base featuring many Fortune 500 companies.

The author of the debut poetry book Dreamland Somewhere Else, Neil describes the collection of poetry as a story of self-discovery and betterment. Neil began writing poetry as a medium of exploring his own thoughts and actions, and trying to gain an understanding on a deeper level into his own interpretation of the meaning of life. This book is a two-year long passion project, that is both autobiographical, and healing.

Follow Neil on social media under the username @bruthaniall.

24166722R00071

Printed in Great Britain
by Amazon